Autumn

LABURNUM
PRESS

Stephen White-Thomson

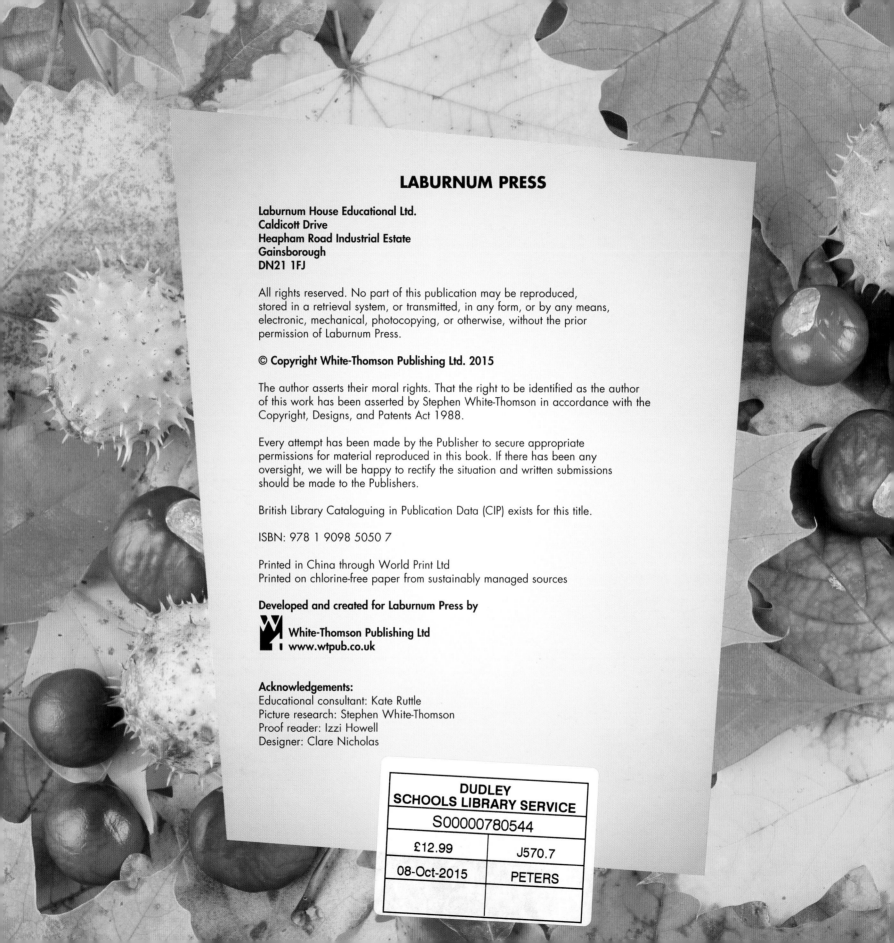

LABURNUM PRESS

Laburnum House Educational Ltd.
Caldicott Drive
Heapham Road Industrial Estate
Gainsborough
DN21 1FJ

British Library Cataloguing in Publication Data (CIP) exists for this title.

ISBN: 978 1 9098 5050 7

Printed in China through World Print Ltd
Printed on chlorine-free paper from sustainably managed sources

Developed and created for Laburnum Press by

White-Thomson Publishing Ltd
www.wtpub.co.uk

Acknowledgements:
Educational consultant: Kate Ruttle
Picture research: Stephen White-Thomson
Proof reader: Izzi Howell
Designer: Clare Nicholas

Contents

Autumn Weather

hat

scarf

gloves

In autumn, the weather becomes cooler and wetter.

What do you need to wear
when it rains hard?

Changing colours

This is a tree in summer.

This is a tree in autumn.

What's happened to the leaves?

Autumn leaves

In America, autumn is called fall.

Why do you think autumn is called fall?

9

Autumn harvest

Apples become ripe

in autumn.

You can pick

them off trees.

Stretch!

10

Can you name some of these harvest fruit and vegetables?

Autumn celebrations

What do you do when it's Halloween?

pumpkin

Autumn festivals

The Hindu festival of Divali is celebrated in autumn.

diva

rangoli

Jewish people eat apples and honey to celebrate Rosh Hashanah.

15

On the farm

Tractors plough the fields.

Farmers plant seeds.

Moo!

munch!

hay

Cows are moved into cowsheds to keep warm.

Autumn seeds

Which trees do these

seeds grow into?

acorn

These conkers grow on horse-chestnut trees.

Autumn animals

Hedgehogs eat lots of food before they hibernate in winter.

In autumn, squirrels bury nuts.

They dig them up during the winter.

Notes for adults

Sparklers books are designed to support and extend the learning of young children. Regular winners of Practical Pre-School silver and gold awards, the books' high-interest subjects link to the Early Years curriculum and beyond. Find out more about Early Years foundation stages (EYFS) at www.gov.uk/government/publications/early-years-foundation-stage-framework–2, and reading with children from the National Literacy Trust (www.literacytrust.org.uk).

Themed titles
Autumn is one of four **Seasons** titles that encourage children to learn about the fun and informative aspects of their lives in the different seasons. The other titles are **Winter** (ISBN: 978 1 9098 5051 4), **Spring** (ISBN: 978 1 9098 5048 4) and **Summer** (ISBN: 978 1 9098 5049 1)

The prime areas of learning: (taught in nurseries)
- communication and language
- physical development
- personal, social and emotional development

The specific areas of learning: (taught in reception classes)
- literacy
- mathematics
- understanding the world
- expressive arts and design

Making the most of reading time
When reading with younger children, take time to explore the pictures together. Ask children to find, identify and count or describe different objects. Point out colours and textures. Allow quiet spaces in your reading so that children can ask questions or repeat your words. Try pausing mid-sentence so that children can predict the next word. This sort of participation develops early reading skills.

Follow the words with your finger as you read. The main text is in Infant Sassoon, a clear, friendly font designed for children learning to read and write. The label and sound effects add fun and give the opportunity to distinguish between levels of communication. Where appropriate, labels, sound effects or main text may be presented phonetically. Encourage children to imitate the sounds.

As you read the book, you can also take the opportunity to talk about the book itself with appropriate vocabulary such as "page", "cover", "back", "front", "label" and "page number".

You can also extend children's learning by using the books as a springboard for discussion and further activities. There are a few suggestions on the facing page.